S0-ARX-430

As White as Snow

by Violet Richards

PEARSON

Glenview, Illinois • Boston, Massachusetts • Chandler, Arizona
Upper Saddle River, New Jersey

snow

Snow is falling outside!
Snow is white.
The land looks white.

Does snow help animals hide?
The polar bear is as white as snow.
Can you find the polar bear?

The little fox is as white as snow.
Can you find the fox?

snowy owl

A snowy owl is as white as snow.
Can you find the snowy owl?

weasel

This weasel is white and black.
Can you find the weasel?

rabbit

The rabbit is as white as snow.
Can you find the rabbit?

The snow is white.
These animals are as white as snow.
These animals can hide
in the snow.